Bridgeport Memories

A special collection of people's
photos and memories of the
"Old Neighborhood"

_____

John McKenzie

Bridgeport Memories
Copyright © 2011 by John McKenzie

Printed in USA by 48HrBooks (www.48HrBooks.com)

Preface

Every few years our church does a fundraiser of some kind to help fund our programs. Many in Bridgeport have enjoyed our Bridgeport-opoly game that was produced twice in the last ten years. This year we thought it would be interesting to make a book about Bridgeport, specifically about people's memories of growing up in the area. The book became much more than a fundraiser. It became a living and breathing story of people's past. In fact, due to the cost of publishing the book, the fundraising part became secondary to the joy of putting it together. We hope this book blesses many for years to come!

Before you begin the journey into the past, I must warn that the memories in this book often expand beyond the geographical borders of Bridgeport to include the following: the Armour Square side of the Canal viaduct, the Chinatown side of 26th street and, even the Canaryville side of Pershing Road. These are all special places that made up the Old Neighborhood, places that will never be forgotten, as long as we have…

"Bridgeport Memories"

<u>Chicago History Museum</u>
By: James Rodgers (cropped)

"Too many people grow up. That's the real trouble with the world, too many people grow up. They forget. They don't remember what it's like to be twelve years old...."
Walt Disney

Introduction

Over the years, I've heard many stories from long time residents of the Bridgeport area about places, events and people. I've always thought it would be great to have a book that would recall all of these things. I thought somebody should write these memories down and gather some pictures before it's all gone.

The good Lord didn't give me many talents, but He did give me two, the ability to listen and a big mouth! I combined my two great talents by listening to stories and retelling them in this book. This is not a history book about Bridgeport, although there is some historical information scattered throughout. It's a simple collection of memories from people that have grown up in the Bridgeport area.

I have to confess that I am not a native Bridgeporter, but a transplanted one. However, I have grown to love this area. It is one of most unique communities in Chicago. I am amazed to see how many generations of families are still connected to this neighborhood. It is interesting to note how everybody seems to know everybody despite living in a big city.

Again, this is not an all inclusive book about the history of Bridgeport, nor could it ever begin to mention all places and institutions that have been here throughout the years. I will leave that to someone else. This is a simple collection of cherished memories, *"**Bridgeport Memories**"*.

Enjoy!

John McKenzie

"I'd give all the wealth that years have piled, the slow result of life's decay, to be once more a little child on a bright summer day" – Lewis Carroll

Chapter One

Bridgeport Eating

Most memories of growing up in Bridgeport center around eating. Many lifelong friendships were built through hours of socializing at neighborhood restaurants and food stands.

If you wanted fancy, you would go to the Governors Table or Mr. Christopher's. If you wanted less formal, you went to David's or Ed's Snack Shop. For pizza you could go to a couple of small stands called Ricobene's or Connie's. Where would you go for ice cream? How about Drexel's on 30th and Shields?

If you were a teen, you could be found hanging out at Augie's. These and many more eating places provide a rich memory for those who grew up in Bridgeport.

A few establishments like the Bridgeport Restaurant and the Ramova Grill have survived the test of time and have been around for decades. Others, such as Connie's and Ricobene's, have even expanded since their inception.

"There were great places to eat on almost every street."

"Anyone remember Bob and Lucy's?
They had the best poorboy sandwiches."

"Bob and Lucy's was a wonderful place. I remember the wooden floors, barrels of olives, and salami that hung from the ceiling."

"Friday nights we used to all hang out at the original Connie's on 26th street."

"At Brent's you could get 3 hamburgers for a buck, but the Shack had the BEST greasy hamburgers around!"

"Kim's Drive In on 26th and Union was close to my house so we'd always get hot dogs, hamburgers, and steak sandwiches. I remember listening to Cassius Clay win the Boxing title there."

"Augie's was the place to go as teens. We would pack the place, eating fries while listening to the juke box."

"We hung at Augie's for 4 generations where we played pinball, listened to the juke box, and smoked our brains out without any adult making us stop."

"There was a place on 31st and Lowe, 'Bosses', where you could get a hotdog, chili, pop, candy etc. It was like a 7/11 without the lottery."

"The Ramova Grill opened in 1929 and is still going strong!"

"I have good memories of going to the Ramova Grill with my brothers and sisters."

"There ain't no other restaurant that can make Chili like the Ramova Grill, it is the GREATEST!"

The Original Ricobene Stand in 1946

Courtesy of Ricobene's

"At the Ricobene's stand, the steak sandwiches were so big we would buy one steak sandwich and a couple of red gravy specials and make 3 or 4 sandwiches out of one!"

"We'd walk from 33rd to 26th just for a greasy bag of fries loaded with ketchup from Ricobene's."

"Neisner's Dime store had great pizza. You could watch the lady making it through the window."

"Remember Winslow Chicken on Racine? You had to bypass the tavern in the front and go to the side door to pick up the BEST chicken around!"

"Remember the Horizon restaurant? It had great BLT sandwiches and mini juke boxes on every table."

"Healthy Foods was around for a long time. I loved their blueberry dumplings."

"Healthy Foods had a delicious sauerkraut soup. It sounds gross but was actually REALLY good!"

"Granata Bakery on Halsted made the BEST Italian Bread! But Dressel's Bakery on 33rd and Wallace was the only place to go for cakes."

"I remember at Dressel's Bakery. There would always be a long line and you had to take a number. I would watch the lady pull string from the ceiling and snap it around your box. I was really surprised when Dressel's closed."

"I lived right above Dressel's Bakery. It always smelled so delicious! Sometimes I would stand by the kitchen door and they would give me sweet rolls."

"My Uncle was the Manager at Dressel's. Whenever there was a birthday in our house, I would go there and he'd give me a cake."

"I loved Cardinale's cannolis and their Italian cookies."

"Remember Kunka's drug store and Ice cream parlor? We would hang out there and try to meet girls. We also loved when the older girls from Inland Steel would go into Betty's Hotdogs (also known as Johnny the Roach) on Archer and Bonfield."

"Cutie Pie on 31st had the best milk shakes and Tasty Freeze had the best chocolate dipped cones."

"I loved Drexel's ice cream on Shields. It was the only place you could get hand dipped ice cream cones."

"Drexel's was connected to the main factory. I used to go in and buy pints for myself instead of cones."

"The Blue Moon was an ice cream shop on 35th and Halsted. My dad would find any excuse to go there. The ice cream selections were based on the Zodiac. My favorite was Virgo. His favorite was the Galaxy, which was HUGE! He and my older sister would share it and always fight for the last spoonful."

"David's had great ice cream too. I remember something called the 'GOLIATH'. I swear it was like three feet tall!"

"I remember as a young girl always getting Eskimo Waffles at David's. I thought I was getting away with something ordering a waffle when I really only wanted the ice cream and topping."

"I always liked looking at the GIANT taffy apples in the window at David's but could never afford to buy one."

*"I loved the huge taffy apples from David's.
They were the size of cantaloupes!"*

"I thought it was so neat how the sidewalk sparkled in front of David's."

"I was thrilled to see the White Sox players eating breakfast there on Sunday mornings."

*"David's was a big part of my life. I was a waitress there. The counter at David's was a place men would spend literally hours drinking coffee and socializing. I served Kevin Bell and Stan Williams from the White Sox, but most importantly...
I met my husband there!"*

*"Me and my husband always ordered the same thing at David's...
Route 66 Steak Burger!"*

"We used to skip mass and go to David's restaurant. We would say we went to St. David's."

"My husband and I heard it on the police scanner first, 'Fire in the Exhaust - DAVID'S Restaurant' We rushed down to see it burning."

"I lived across the street from David's and couldn't believe the flames coming out of it!"

David's Restaurant and the Governor's Table 1972

Chicago History Museum, By: Joseph G. Domin, 1972

"I was a cheerleader at St. Mary's of P.H. and after every basketball game we would go to the Governor's Table whether we won or lost. I loved the Vanilla Cokes!"

14

The Stockyard Inn in the 1950's

"You could brand your own steak at the Stock Yard Inn"

The Winery on 31st and Wells 1970

"My Mother worked at the Winery. We used to get gravy specials at the side window for like a dime. You could get red or brown."

Mr. Christopher's 26th and Normal 1966

Chicago History Museum by: Sigmund J. Osty (cropped)

Courtesy of Jimmy Cos

"The original Hickory Pit was on 28th and Emerald.
They had good RIBS!"

The original Johnny O's on 31st 1972

Chicago History Museum, By:Joseph C. Domin

ART'S Hotdog Stand 31st and Morgan 1970

Chicago History Museum, By:Casey Prunchunas

Although there were many great hot dog stands in Bridgeport, 'Mike the Hot Dog Man' on 32nd place and Aberdeen was probably the most famous stand. He sold hot dogs and tamales in Bridgeport for 65 years.

According to his daughter Diana, Michael Knabjian was originally from Turkey. He came to Chicago in 1920 and sold hotdogs from a box on his back throughout the neighborhood until 1935 when he set up a cart on Aberdeen.

*"We got hotdogs all the time from Mike.
The line was always long, but it was worth the wait!"*

Ed's Snack Shop 1972

*"Ed's Snack Shop was at one time
the Friars Kitchen and later Sophie's."*

Georges Café 3465 S. Morgan 1966

Eating Places Gone But Still Remembered

Arts Hot Dog
Augie's
The Blue Moon
Bob and Lucy's
Brent's Hamburgers
Bosses
Cutie Pie
David's
Del Mar's
Dorio's Restaurant
Dressel's Bakery
Drexel Ice Cream
Ed's Snack Shop
Goliath's Burgers
Governors Table
Healthy Foods
The Horizon
The Hickory Pit
Jack's Burgers
Kim's Drive In
Michalski Bakery
Mr. Christopher's
Tastee Freeze
The Shack
The Winery
Winslow's Chicken

And So Many More...

Chapter Two

Bridgeport Theatres

Probably the best known theatre in Bridgeport was the Ramova on Halsted Street. It was a place where your feet could stick to the floor, you could smoke in the lobby and you could see Humphrey Bogart or John Wayne in action. However, the Ramova was not the only theatre in Bridgeport, there were several others.

The Wallace Theatre located at Wallace and 31st street, was running until the mid 1960's. The Butler theatre was located on 26th street near Wallace. It became the Norwal theatre until it was phased out in the 1950's. The Eagle was located at 33rd place and Morgan and it also closed in the 50's. The original buildings for the Eagle and Wallace theatres are still intact.

The Milda theatre was located on South Halsted and seated around 900. All of these interesting facts were found on the web site for Cinema Treasures. The following is a list of Bridgeport theaters from the Cinema Treasure listings:

Bridgeport/Holden Theatre – 2839 South Archer: 1910-1950's
Butler /Norwal Theatre – 518 West 26th Street: 1913-1950's
Casino Theatre – 3508 South Halsted: 1920's-1940's
Eagle Theatre -3324 South Morgan: 1915 - 1950's
Loomis Theatre – 2858 South Archer: 1913-1950's
Marion Theatre – 3446 South Halsted: 1920's
Milda Theatre – 3140 South Halsted: 1914-1950's
Monogram Theatre – 3520 South Halsted: 1900-1920's
Ramova Theatre – 3518 South Halsted:1929-1980's
Wallace Theatre – 624 West 31st Street: 1912-1966

Ramova Theatre 3518 S. Halsted 1954

Chicago History Museum, Photographer: Lil and Al Bloom

"I remember going to the Ramova on Saturday afternoons. Popcorn would be flying through the air, and kids screaming throughout the whole movie."

"For 25 cents you saw two movies and a cartoon at the Ramova. For another quarter you could get a pop and popcorn or redhots."

"I loved the stars on the ceiling that would sparkle and glow."

"I once lost the heel from my black dress shoes when it stuck to the floor at the Ramova."

22

"The girl's bathroom was pink and it was the place to smoke as a kid. I think all the smoke actually helped cover the nasty smell of urinal cakes."

"One time I saw a water bug as BIG as my FINGER!"

"One could never forget the smell of popcorn as you enter the show and the mice running across your feet!"

"We used to call it the RATmova."

"Remember George the usher? He carried a flash light, wore an extra wide 5" tie and always had a cigar butt hanging out of his mouth as he'd try to quiet everyone down."

"The Ramova was the most popular show to see the most recent movies. The BLOB was one of the scariest movies I ever saw there!"

"My dad took me and my sister to see Jaws. During one of the scariest scenes, a hand reached out and grabbed my sister's shoulder. It was our neighbor sitting behind us. It gave her nightmares for months."

"After seeing Jaws at the Ramova, I woke up screaming thinking my sister had been eaten alive because all I could see was her head sticking out of a red blanket."

"The Ramova was the dating place for many."

"I met my husband at the Ramova."

"In 1964 the Beatles movie 'Hard Day's Night' played at the Ramova. I remember being part of the packed house. We girls were out of our minds screaming and crying. I stayed for THREE showings!"

"They sometimes had special appearances from actors in the movies at the Ramova. I remember a giant that came. He played a giant in the movie and he looked like a giant in person."

"The Ramova had a promotion for a James Bond movie and the guy who played the "Jaws" character was there to sign autographs."

"I think the last movie I saw at the Ramova Theatre was Conan the Barbarian"

Norwal Theatre 518 w. 26th Street

"The Norwal was a small one aisle theatre with good popcorn."

*"The Wallace theater was small but cheap.
You could get in for a dime."*

*"Remember how you would get gifts at the Wallace,
like a towel or dish to take home?"*

*"At the Wallace, when you looked to your side, you did not know if
you were going to see your friend sitting next to you, or a RAT!"*

"I remember rats were as big as cats at the Wallace Theatre."

*"I had so much fun with my sister and her friends when we saw
'Hard Day's Night' at the Wallace. At the end of the movie they
were up in front of the big screen pretending they were the Beatles.
It was the coolest thing I'd ever seen."*

*"Every Tuesday I went to the Metropole theatre with my
grandmother for our special day out, but also because they gave
out free gifts. I actually still have some of the
dishes they gave out."*

Courtesy of Barbara Alberts

Chicago History Museum (cropped)

*"The building next to the Winery used to be the Metropole Theatre.
The story goes that Miss Val, a downtown nightclub dancer,
married the owner of the Metropole, Edward Brunnel. She turned
the theatre into a Dance Studio after his death in the 1950's. If you
look closely you will see the two white boards that always had
pictures of the girls in their tutu's."*

*"I took dance lessons from Ms. Val year after year. She was a
wonderful dancer and teacher. Miss Val put on great dance
recitals from the 1950's until 1991."*

Chapter Three

<u>Bridgeport Parks & Recreation</u>

In the early 1900's Chicago embarked on a campaign to provide social places and recreational opportunities for various Chicago neighborhoods. Two of the first ten parks were Armour Square and Mark White. Mark White is now known as McGuane Park. The two parks had a profound influence on the building of parks in the United States. Many Bridgeport residents have fond memories of growing up and being involved in various park programs at McGuane, Armour, and other parks and playlots throughout the neighborhood.

<u>Mark White Park</u>

The original name of McGuane Park was Mark White. Mark White had served as a superintendent for the park commission for over two decades.

Mark White became McGuane Park in 1960. The park was named after John McGuane who lived right by the park and was involved for several decades. He also served as a Chicago Park District board commissioner. In the early 70's the current park building was built.

"There was a lot to do at Mark White Park. You could ice skate in the winter and go swimming in the summer."

*"I basically played sports at Mark White twelve hours a day, seven days a week. A big thrill was playing football for the **McGuane Park Steelers** youth football team."*

Mark White Outdoor Pool

Courtesy of McGuane Park

"The pool didn't have a filter so they would close the pool on Wednesdays to drain it and refill it. This is why it was so cold!"

"We use to sneak in at night and go swimming at the outdoor Mark White Pool. That is probably why they built the new one indoors."

"I remember in 1963 a tornado came to the south side and I can still remember all the trees in the park were all over the place."

"The girl's baseball and volleyball teams at Mark White won their share of trophies with the help of Mrs. Green the Park Matron. I remember how she would literally stuff most of us into her car to

take us to away games. She got stopped once by the police for overloading to which she replied, "Do you know who I am?"

*"Ed Kazak, the gym instructor, made you come for **ALL** the activities if you wanted to play basketball. So we had to do everything. He was really the BEST although he'd say, 'not really.' I recently attended his funeral."*

"When they were dedicating McGuane Park in 1960, I was in a 100 yard dash race and won. Minnie Minoso was there and he came over and gave me a baseball."

Armour Square Park

Armour Square opened in 1906 and was named after Philip D. Armour owner of the largest meat packing company in the world. Armour was known for donating a large amount of his fortune to charity.

"Me and my friends always hung out at Armour Park. Most of the Italians hung there."

"There was a lot that went on at Armour Park. The swimming pool was huge and shaped in an 'L'. I also remember winning the city wide volleyball championship in 1967."

"Way back, the De LaSalle high school varsity team use to play their football games at Armour Park."

"Handball was a favorite at Armour. That's all I remember doing when I wasn't getting into trouble."

"In 1968 on the third wooden bench in the lobby of the Armour field house, my future husband asked me to go steady."

"I remember Ms. Jan (Jan Pacente) teaching us at Armour Park. She would do great water ballet shows and teach volleyball. Everyone loved her. I believe the playground is named after her."

"I remember I couldn't wait until I was old enough to join the water ballet team. I was going to be the next Esther Williams, Turned out it was a lot harder than it looked; I nearly drowned!"

Bosley Park

Bosely Park was originally called Holden Park and was built in 1901 to provide a play area for the overcrowded neighborhood around the area. The park name was changed in 1916 to William F. Bosley who donated $9000 to purchase more land for the park.

"After school we'd hang at Bosely. Once I was playing football with the guys trying to show off in front of the girls. I showed a lot more than I anticipated. I jumped up but my pants stayed down. I'm sure there are a few people that still remember that!"

Donovan Park

Donovan Park was built in 1955 and was originally named Sangamon Park. The name was changed in 1959 in remembrance of Chicago fire fighter, Captain George L. Donovan, who was one of three fire fighters that died fighting a blaze in 1957.

"We hung at Donavan playing baseball all day."

Wilson Park

Wilson Park was named after John P. Wilson, a Bridgeport alderman who later became the deputy commissioner of Public Works for more than thirty years. The park was built in the early 1930's and also included the last municipal bath house built by the city. There were at one time, eighteen municipal bath houses in Chicago because so many houses did not have indoor plumbing. The Wilson bath house remained open until 1959.

Public Bath House located at 2839 S. Halsted 1960

<u>Hardin Square Park</u>

Bridgeport residents might also remember Hardin Square Park which was by Chinatown. It was replaced by the Dan Ryan expressway in the 1960's.

"From 1956-1962, I played little league at Hardin Square on 26th and Wentworth. We were city champions. We had 10 different nationalities represented on our team and we were written up in the newspaper."

*"We played little league **at All Saint's Currelli Field** on 25th and Lowe. It was a field of rocks...Ouch!"*

<u>NEIGHBORHOOD FUN</u>

"Summers were the best in Bridgeport. Everyone would be out sitting on their porches until the wee hours of night."

"As kids, we would hang out on the corners or sit on our friend's porches. All the parents knew who you were and were as strict with you as their own kids."

"There was an undeniable bond between everyone."

"We would play in the streets: football, baseball, marbles hide and seek and running bases."

"Do you remember the Lupini man? He'd be pushing his peanut cart down the street during the summer yelling, 'seeds, seeds'."

"The Lupini man sold all kinds of Italian nuts and pumpkin seeds. You could get a 10 cent bag or 25 cent bag."

Courtesy of Anthony Chira (Pump on 27th and Normal)

"Every Fire Hydrant was open in the summer.
We'd all be playing in the water. "

"It seemed like the men would wash their cars everyday in the
hydrant and then go under the viaduct to wax them."

"In the fall came Halloween. Halloween was full of eggs and
shaving cream fights from 26th to 33rd. The cops would be chasing
us all night long! Those were the days!"

DANCING

"We had great street dances and block parties during those times.
I remember everyone, young and old, dancing."

"Every Catholic Church had a teen club and we would have
dances every Friday night."

"The best dances were at All Saints Church. I loved going with my older brother because he wasn't embarrassed to dance with me. We had the jitterbug down!"

"Armour Park often had dance contests. I was in one once. I didn't win even though I was a great dancer. It must have been my partners fault (smile)."

"There was dancing at St. Mary's Gym, Benton House and the New National Ballroom nicknamed, THE BUCKET OF BLOOD!"

"The Harmony club every Friday night had local teen bands play and dance contests."

"I remember a band playing on 26th street called JC and the Apostles."

"I use to be a 'Go Go' dancer for JC and the Apostles."

"Santa Maria Incoronata on 25th place had great dances with live bands."

"I would go to the Harmony Club to watch my future husband play in his band. (He didn't know I was watching him.)"

BOWLING

"It seemed like every area had a bowling alley and a movie theatre."

"I can remember a few bowling alleys. There was Milo's near 35th and Halsted. They had an alley on the second floor. There was also Johnny Walls which was a small 6 lane alley that actually had pin boys setting the pins."

"I had my first brush with crime at Milo's – somebody stole my father's bowling ball!"

"The Lithuanian Hall had bowling in the basement and Archer and Loomis Bowl was above the bar."

"The Harmony Club had a three lane bowling alley."

The Lithuanian Dance Hall (The Harmony Club) 31st and Halsted

Courtesy of Photographer: Gene Pesek

"We'd also go to St. Barbara's social center to bowl. It had a 6 lane bowling alley."

"Remember bowling with pin setters near 26th and Wentworth? It took FOREVER!"

"Every Sunday after 9:00 am mass at St. Jerome, we would bowl at Renzino's Bowl on 25th and Wentworth.
It was only 50 cents a game."

"I believe Renzino's Bowl and the Ten Pin Lounge was owned by Doctor Renzino."

"I was on a bowling league at Renzino's Bowl. Everyone wanted me on their team not for my great bowling skill, but rather for my lack thereof. I was given a trophy for most gutter balls."

"Our school league bowled at IIT. The lanes weren't so great, but we loved it! We would wear the same color shirts to show what team we were on and all walk together to IIT."

"I lovingly remember Nap's bowl on 26th street. I loved the smell of the bowling alley. It felt like home."

"Nap's was a fun place to bowl. For years they had grade school leagues that many of us were part of."

Naponiello's Bowl on 26th Street

Chapter Four

Bridgeport Schools & Churches

Memories of school can be sweet or sour. Many Bridgeport kids went to parochial schools which were in abundance in the area. St. Bridget, St. George, St. Mary, Nativity, St. Barbara, and St. Jerome are just a few of the Catholic schools that have been here throughout the years. Thousands of kids have been taught by nuns and priests.

Along with the private schools, there were also many school memories from public schools such as: Mark Sheridan, Armour, Holden, Healey, Ward, and McClellan. One thing is for sure, whether it was public school or Catholic school, school day memories abound!

"I remember at St. Jerome being taught by strict nuns wearing black habits."

"I had the legendary meanest nun in the history of St. Jerome's School not only in first grade, but again in sixth grade. Anyone remember Sister Lucille? [God rest her soul]"

"I went to St. David on 32nd and Emerald. I have wonderful memories of Father Boyle and Father Thomas. I still have many friends today from that time."

"I remember at St. David's School, Sister Marie would always sprinkle us with Holy Water as she left the room. I always got the bulk of it because I sat by the door. Maybe that's why I turned out so good!"

Holden School 1907

Chicago History Museum, Photographer: Chicago Daily News

"I went to Holden School. I can still remember the route I used to walk; out the back gate, down the alley, through a maze of gangways and empty lots until I reached the school. I can't IMAGINE any kid being ALLOWED to do that TODAY!"

"I had my freshmen year of high school at Holden School."

"I went to St. Mary's of Perpetual Help from 1st grade all the way through High School. High School was so much fun that I was never tempted to ditch school. I made LIFELONG friends."

"I went to St. Mary's of Perpetual Help. We were all taught by nuns in their eighties! If you were sick and missed school, they would always say it was because you did not wear your BUBUSHKA scarf."

St. Mary's High School 1950's

Chicago History Museum

"I used to go see my cousin in all the Polish dances at St, Mary's."

"My funniest memory of St. Mary's High School is when my husband (friend at that time) came in pretending he was a photographer and asked for someone to show him around. We went through the school taking pretend pictures and then we snuck out for lunch."

"At Immaculate Conception grammar school, we'd fast from midnight to 8am for first Friday mass. After mass we could buy egg sandwiches from the Sisters of St. Francis of Assisi. I loved those egg sandwiches on white bread!"

"I went to All Saints grammar school. I remember when West Side Story came out and all the guys in the class would walk down the street snapping their fingers."

"I went to St. John of Nep at 30th and Lowe. The Nuns lived at the school so there was NEVER a snow day. I still keep in touch with the kids I went to school with."

"I went to Ward school so I would pal around with my friends from 24th street and hang out in Chinatown. There was always something to do in Chinatown."

"I went to Webster School on 33rd and Wentworth. One of my fondest memories is when the boy behind me dipped my curls into the ink well. I had ink all over my dress. My mom wasn't too happy and the boy got into trouble and never forgave me."

Armour School Kindergarten Graduation 1957

Chicago History Museum

Bridgeport Churches

Religion was important to the Bridgeport Community and churches were found in abundance. For most, parish life was an important part of growing up in Bridgeport. Many churches are still here though some are now gone.

St George was located at Lithuanica and 33rd street and was one of the first Lithuanian Catholic churches built in the United States. Amazingly, St. George's school at one time had almost 1,000 students attending! The school building is still standing and is presently used by Armour school.

St. Bridget was located on Archer Avenue. In the 1940's and 50's, St. Bridget had several thousand attend mass on weekends. Both of these churches were gone by the early 1990's.

St. Bridget

Nativity of Our Lord is one of the oldest churches in Chicago, being started in 1868 to meet the needs of the Irish living in Bridgeport. A few years later, St. Gabriel was founded in 1881 to also meet the spiritual needs of Irish families.

St. Jerome was founded in 1912 to meet the spiritual needs of the Croatians in Bridgeport. St. Mary of Perpetual Help was founded in 1882 to meet the needs of the Polish. St. Barbara was founded in 1909 to relieve the crowding conditions of St. Mary's. Both structures, which were built a few years after each church was founded, are magnificent additions to the Bridgeport skyline.

Of course, protestant churches were also a part of Bridgeport though there were fewer. Doremus Congregational Church was on Normal Avenue for almost 100 years before becoming New Life Bridgeport.

First Lutheran church of Trinity is one of the oldest churches in Bridgeport being established in 1865. Holy Cross Lutheran church was organized in 1886. In addition, you had a small church on 31st street called Raymond Chapel which is now Central Assembly of God.

Raymond Chapel 1966 – Now Central Assembly of God

Chicago History Museum **Photographer: Sigmund Osty**

"The churches in Bridgeport seemed to be attended by people of specific nationalities. I Attended St. Mary's with many Polish people."

"St. Jerome's Croatian church had the most beautiful Christmas Midnight Mass."

"I would always pretend to put money in the candle stand at St. Jerome's by tapping my ring to make noise just so I could light a candle."

"I use to ring the bells for St. Jerome at noon, 6pm and for every Sunday Mass. It was hard with 2 ropes and 2 bells on Sundays."

"Remember when you had to wear scarves or doilies on your heads at mass?"

"My mom said that if you didn't have a scarf, the nuns would bobby pin a tissue to your head."

Nativity Rosary Club

Courtesy of Nadine Pajauskas Downs

43

"There was a time you had to pay a dime to save a seat at mass."

"I skipped mass for so long that when I decided to go one Sunday, I handed the usher a dime for my seat and he chased me down the aisle to return my dime. He said they stopped doing that over a year ago. Had it been that long? How Embarrassing! My sisters had a field day with that one."

"All Saints on 25th and Wallace was beautiful until the expressway came through and took so many parishes away."

"I was married at Santa Maria Incoronata"

"I always loved stopping to pray to 'Our Lady' in the Gratto outside of St. George's Church."

"I have fond memories of Doremus Church. Even though I was Catholic, I would sneak to see Rev. Morris who taught me all about the Bible and Jesus. He gave me my first Bible. I still have it all tattered and written in."

"Being raised Catholic; I was hesitant to visit Central Assembly on 31st and Poplar. When I finally decided to go, I actually made my husband wait outside in the car just in case I wanted to run out. That was over 25 years ago and I keep running back."

St. George Church

Chicago History Museum

St. George Carnival – 1960's

"St. George had a big carnival every year with great rides. A LOT of people attended and went on those rides."

"I remember standing in line at St. George's carnival to buy Kugelis!"

"Santa Maria Incoronata always had great carnivals. I remember one year, my dad let one of the game booths set up in front of our house."

"At Santa Maria Incoronata's Carnival, there was a big stage and bands would play. Me and my friend would pretend we were conducting the band while waving our cannoli as conductor sticks. The inevitable happened; the cannoli filling flew out of the shell and onto a man's shirt! Oops!"

"August 15th means the Feast of the Assumption (Velika Gospa) at St. Jerome Church. After the procession, there was food and a festival all day long."

"Processions have been a special part of Bridgeport for generations; St. Rocco, St. Joseph and the Blessed Mother."

"The fireworks were so LOUD and the processions would always end with a carnival."

"St. Rocco would be draped with money that people would donate as you passed their houses. The band would play loudly when a large donation was given."

"They would end the St. Rocco Processions by firing off a block long string of firecrackers."

"We would spend days decorating   our Candle Shrines."
(La Gendas)

St. Joseph Day Procession on 26ᵗʰ near Dalcamo

Courtesy of Frankie Chira

"Did anyone have the traveling Virgin stay at their home? The Blue Army would bring the statue of the Blessed Mother to your home and you would allow people to come in and say the rosary each day."

"My Grandmother always hosted the traveling Virgin near Christmas. I remember they had us kids saying the Rosary on Christmas Eve just to keep us busy while Santa Clause was setting up our presents. When we heard Santa's bell ring, everything went flying out of our hands, prayer sheets everywhere. I can still feel the excitement!"

"When we were little, we had the traveling Virgin at our home. My mom would have cake and coffee each night for the people that would come to pray. One night she sent my younger brother to the store to buy napkins. I'll never forget what he pulled out of the bag. He didn't buy just ordinary napkins, he got SANITARY napkins. 60 years later and we still won't let him live it down."

"There is a time for everything.....a time to be born and a time to die, a time to plant and time to uproot, a time to kill and a time to heal, a time tear down, a time to build, a time to weep and a time to laugh, a time to mourn and a time to dance...a time to keep and a time to throw away..." Ecclesiastes 3

Chapter Five

Bridgeport Businesses and Organizations

Bridgeport is still known today for its family owned businesses that have been passed down through the generations. There are still some businesses that are still around after many decades such as the following: The Bridgeport News, Pulaski Savings, Dalcamo's Funeral Home, Bernice's Tavern, Bridgeport Bakery, Colleta's Funeral Home, and several others.

Looking East from Emerald on 26th Street in 1942

Chicago History Museum

It is a known fact that immigrants found solace in churches and saloons. Bridgeport had a surplus of both!

P. O'Neills Whiskies 33rd and Halsted in the 1890's

G.A. Regan 3459 S. Halsted in the 1890's

Chicago History Museum

Pomierski Funeral Home, corner of 32ⁿᵈ and Aberdeen in the early 1920's.

"This was when visitations were still held in the families' homes."

"Pomierski Funeral home is one of the oldest family run businesses in Bridgeport that is still around today."

1930's Cadillac hearse side loader with electric table.

"Walter Pomierski was one of the first to own a side loader hearse."

Walter Pomierski Sr. in 1940

Courtesy of Pomierski Funeral Home

"Everyone dressed well during these days. The grave diggers even wore uniforms back then."

Dalcamo Funeral Home 1966
Family owned and operated since 1939

Chicago History Museum by: Sigmund J. Osty (cropped)

700 W. 31st 1966

Chicago History Museum By:Sigmund J. Osty (cropped below)

If you look closely, you can see the original
Blake and Lamb Funeral Home.

Corner Stores

Ralph's 519 W. 26th Street

Courtesy of Frankie Chira

"I remember as a kid always going to the Corner Store for candy. There were "Corner Stores" all over the neighborhood."

"My favorites were Rogers candy store on 31st and Morgan and Kelly's Candy Store on 32nd and Morgan."

"There was Palmarius where you could get the stalest candies around. That's why you could get a whole bag for 5 cents. You could also get a sour pickle with a peppermint stick stuck in the middle. YUK! (or maybe Yum! depending on what you like.)"

*"Remember TOOTY's Corner on 28th and Princeton? There was a
book written by a neighbor about the guys who hung there."*

"I was just invited to go see a play about Tooty's Corner."

Ralph Vacarro Grocery 519 W. 26th Street

Courtesy of Anthony Chira

*"My grandparents owned Ralph Vaccaro's store on 26th. The
paper in the middle of the table is where they killed the chickens
and rabbits and wrapped them to go."*

"I worked at Tony's Grocery Store on 31st."

*"Tony's was open 365 days a week. When he felt like it
he'd make deals with you."*

*"Certified Foods once had the Weiner Mobile. Little Oscar and
Henry Height were there too!"*

Gibby's Food was on 36th and Parnell for 40 years.

"Gibby was my dad, Gilbert Pajauskas and he owned the store until the day he died. My dad ground his own meat, made his own sausage and prepared a traditional Lithuanian dish called kugelis. He had customers who long ago left the neighborhood but would make the trip back to purchase a pan of kugelis for special occasions."

"On December 23, 1994 Gibby passed away. He had just finished making a pan of kugelis and had sat down in his rocking chair in the store to relax. A customer had found him a short time later. On Christmas day our family shared the last pan of kugelis he ever made. It was a bittersweet day but a very special memory of my father and his little store that was such an important part of our family and of our neighborhood."

Schulze and Burch Biscuit Co. 1133 W. 35th St. 1940's

Courtesy of Oscar & Associates, Inc.

REMEMBER TOAST'EMS?

The Schulze and Burch Biscuit Co. was built in the 1930's at 1135 W. 35th street. This is where the first toaster pastry, Toast'ems, was created in 1964. That is why many referred to it as the 'Pop Tart factory'. They also created the first granola bar and dual texture cookie at this plant.

The company was responsible for producing the Butternut bread and Flavor Kist cookie brands. It even revolutionized saltine crackers by making them thinner and packaging them in four wraps in one carton. All this info and more can be found on the Schulze and Burch website.

"We loved the outlet store they used to have. The Flavor Kist butter cookies were one of my favorites. We'd put them on our fingers like rings and eat around them."

33rd Place and Halsted 1970

Chicago History Museum By: Sigmund Osty

Atlas Uniform Company 3130 S. Halsted 1972

Chicago History Museum , By: Joseph Domin

1032 w. 32nd Place 1904

Chicago History Museum By: Joseph Domin

34th and Halsted 1971

Chicago History Museum , By:Casey Prunchunas

The Livery on 41st and Halsted 1964

Chicago History Museum by: Casey Prunchunas

*"In our backyard we had a place to tie up horses. I asked my dad
'Why would we had this in our backyard?' and he said,
'Cause I had horses at one time. This was how we got around.'
I just never pictured my dad riding a horse."*

Organizations

Through the many years there have been several organizations in Bridgeport that have served literally thousands of Bridgeporters in a variety of ways. The Benton House, Fellowship House, Italian American Club, and Valentine's Boy and Girls Clubs are just some of the fine organizations that have been a part of Bridgeport for many decades.

The Valentine Girl's Club 1973

Chicago History Museum By: Casey Prunchunas (cropped)

"The Girls club had great shows. I can still remember the song we danced to…"Got a go now, got a hit the road…"

"After watching one of the shows at the Valentine's club, I told my kindergarten teacher at St. Jerome that I took tap there. She had me dance at my graduation. I had never tap danced in my life, but that didn't stop me. I'm not sure what I really did but my grandfather said I almost killed him. He had the "Death Laugh".

"The Boys club was better because they had the pool and all the dances were held in their gym."

Chapter Six

Bridgeport Shopping

Though Bridgeport is not a major shopping center now, many remember when Bridgeport had a variety of businesses and shopping places that were able to meet local needs. You could find clothing, shoes, furniture, gas, groceries, bakeries and much more.

For several decades until the 1950's, Halsted street was known in some quarters as the "Lithuanian downtown" because of several businesses that were started by and catered to the large group of Lithuanians that lived in Bridgeport. Most of the businesses are now long gone, but many still live in memory.

Archer Avenue 1880's

Chicago History Museum

35th and Halsted 1970

Chicago History Museum, By: Sigmund J. Osty (cropped)

"Sally Ann's at 35th and Halsted was for women and next door was Norman's for men."

"When I was younger, I was always with my mom and her lady friends. I loved to drink tea with them. One day, we went to Sally's Lingerie Shop and I was shocked to see all these women topless getting measured for bras. I believe that scarred me for life!"

"Remember how all the guys wore the same pants and shirts just in different colors? My brothers had to have Sansabelt pants and shirts with a collar that looked like bowling shirts."

"I remember going to Petries and trying on clothes in the aisles. (no dressing room). You could get an outfit for $20.00 and then go next door to Boston's for a pair of shoes. You were now set for the BIG dance!"

"There used to be two five and dime stores on 34th and Halsted;
Becks and KB department stores."

"Woolworth's was the dime store I remember. As a kid my aunt
brought me in there and I got to sit on the tall stool at the counter
and eat right in the store!"

Weller's Department store 32nd and Morgan Street 1972

<u>**Chicago History Museum**</u> **By: Casey Prunchunas**

"Remember Weller's Department Store?"

"*I loved to look at all the stuff they had in the windows.***"**

Spiegel Outlet 35th and Racine 1963

Chicago History Museum , by: Casey Prunchunas, (cropped)

"How about Spiegel's Outlet Store? I loved it! The wood floors, the big elevator, and if you could find something you liked, the price was right."

"The Spiegel's warehouse was one of the scariest buildings to be in. It was an old rickety building with a big service elevator that a man would run."

"The first time I went to Spiegel's, I thought they were having a 'going out of business sale' because of the set up and the mark downs. I was trying to get all the deals I could before it went out of business. It was around for a long time before it really went out of business. I miss it especially around Christmas time."

Standard Gas Station on 26th and Canal 1966

Chicago History Museum by: Sigmund J. Os (cropped)

"Businesses always had promotions and gifts. I got my whole set of CHINA from the GAS STATION. Every time you filled up, you got stickers that you could cash in for pieces."

Can't forget S&H green stamps!

Courtesy of Nadine Pajauskas Downs

"Once I had my brother pose as my husband to earn three books of S&H green stamps. We had to sit through a vacuum demonstration. I got enough stamps to get a card table!"

"I got to actually go the S&H Green Stamp store with all of my books."

"Let's not forget the peddlers that came in their horse drawn wagon with fruits and vegetables."

Courtesy of Frankie Chira

"Our neighbor would get a bushel of the bad fruit from him and then cut off the rotten parts and let us kids in the neighborhood eat the good parts. It sounds gross, but it was exciting for us as kids."

"Remember the Pony Pictures? I think every household in the neighborhood had a picture of a kid sitting on the pony."

"People really knew how to make a living back then. Remember the Chicken Man? For a dime he'd make the chicken dance for you."

"No dime, no show."

*"The best were the **Jewish merchants** that came to your house with big catalogues. They had everything from towels to life insurance. My merchant was Mr. Hytoff."*

"Every area had a Jewish Merchant. They were like door to door salesmen that let you buy on a payment plan. I remember my mom hiding once when our Jewish merchant, Ralph, came to collect and she didn't have a payment. She told me to tell him she wasn't home and that is exactly what I said, 'She said to tell you she's not home.' She was so mad at me!"

"There were lots of drug stores in the neighborhood; Super X, Rexall and Holden just to name a few."

"If we were sick, my mothers use to say, "let's go to the doctor." She'd really take us to Holden Drugs and Louie the druggist would prescribe things for us."

"Louie at Holden Drugs created a vitamin for kids that we all had to take."

"Louie the Druggist had an old fashion scale and a two way mirror, he could see out but you couldn't see in. So, if he saw you grab the door knob to come in, he had a way to zap you with a buzzer."

"If too many of us would congregate in front of Holden Drug store, Louie would come out with women's perfume and start spraying us until we ran away."

"We would go to Rexall Drugs on 31st and Wallace for practically everything. I remember Jerry Schwartz was the pharmacist there before he became a doctor and opened his first office on 31st. He put on my first of many casts."

"Remember when doctors made house calls?"

"I remember being so sick once as a kid lying on the couch, so pathetic. All of a sudden, a strange man with a black bag came in and the whole family gathered around as he began to exam me. It scared the beans out of me back then, but how I long for those home visits today when I am sick!"

35th and Halsted 1970

Chicago History Museum by: Sigmund J. Osty (cropped)

30th and Halsted next to Ed's Snack Shop 1972

Chicago History Museum, By: Joseph C. Domin

Businesses Gone But Still Remembered

Berk's Jewelers
Boston Shoes
Community Store
Clothesline
Father and Son's Shoes
Gibby's Grocery
Holden Drugs
Kaplan Shoes
Kelly's Candy Store
K&S Discount Store
L & M Discount Store
Mario's Grocery Store
Melody's Records
Neisner's Dime Story
Norman's Men's Clothing
Oklahoma Gas Station
Petri's Clothes
Ralph's Grocery
Sally Ann's
Spiegel's
Tony's Grocery
Universal Shoes
Weller's Department Store
Wendt's Furniture
Woolworth's Dime Store

And the list goes on…

Chapter Seven

Bridgeport Iconic Places

Growing up in Bridgeport, one was fortunate to have several of Chicago's iconic places right in their own backyard. You had the Amphitheatre, Stockyards, and Sterns Quarry all located on Halsted Street. At 35th and Shields you could find Comiskey Park. Comiskey served pro sports teams and also hosted a variety of special events throughout the years.

The Stockyards

The Union Stock Yards had a major impact on Bridgeport for many decades. Whether it was jobs, the meat you ate, or the unforgettable smell on a warm August night, the Stock Yards were a big part of Bridgeport life. The stockyards were built over a 320 acre swamp land in 1864. Over the years, more acreage was added. By the early 1900's, the stockyards encompassed over 130 miles of railroad track and 50 miles of roads.

It is estimated that at one time, the stockyards produced 80% of the meat eaten in the United States. During WWI, over 9 million pounds of meat a day was being produced! At its peak, over 25,000 people were working in the stockyards. This brought many immigrants to the area such as: Lithuanians, Bohemians, Polish and many others. The dominant meat producers were Armour, Swift, Wilson and Morris. Fires were always a potential hazard and in 1910 a major fire killed 21 firemen.

Sadly, after WW2 as interstate highway travel became much more prominent and vehicle refrigeration became more sophisticated, packing houses started to move to different parts of the country with Omaha, Nebraska becoming a major center. The Union Stockyards, which had served the country for a century, closed down July 30, 1971. Today, the stockyards serve as an industrial park with dozens of businesses. There are few structures left from the stockyards. However, the entrance arch, that has served as a welcome entrance, built in 1879, still stands.

Chicago History Museum, By:Kaufmann & Fabry, 1928

"Who could forget the smell of the stockyards?"

"The smell was so bad I can still smell it today. It's something you NEVER forget!"

"When it was coming to an end, you could see dead cows lying on their backs, legs up, stiff as can be. [Not a pretty memory]"

"I remember when a trailer full of animals was being fixed on 33rd and Wentworth. We blew the locks off and let the cattle loose throughout the neighborhood. We helped get them back to the truck while leaving one out to be slaughtered."
'Where's the beef?'

Courtesy of Fran Sabia

"I remember when the animals got loose from the trailer and showed up in Armour Park."

77

Stearns Quarry

Stearns Quarry, located on Halsted Street near McGuane Park, helped build Chicago with its quality limestone. The Quarry opened in 1836 and was in operation until 1969. It was then used as a landfill for clean construction materials for several decades. The quarry is now a beautiful part of McGuane Park called the Henry C. Palmisano Park.

"Remember the blast from the Quarry? It happened every day at 3pm. Everyone felt it!"

"It always fascinated me to watch the workers down in the Quarry."

"I had some hippie friends that spent their honeymoon night at the bottom of the Quarry."

"Stearns Quarry was constantly dynamiting. The ground would shake and scare everyone."

"They tried to fill the quarry with garbage at one time. It smoldered and the smell filled the whole neighborhood."

"I looked over the edge into the quarry and it took my breath away to see how far down it went."

"There was more down in the Quarry than just limestone. Grandpa never could keep his teeth in his mouth!"

International Amphitheater

The International Amphitheater was built in 1934, by the Stock Yard Co., for a cost of $1.5 million dollars. The main purpose was to host livestock shows. Over the years, the Amphitheatre actually hosted hundreds of different types of events such as the following: auto shows, political conventions, music concerts, circuses, sports, religious events and much more. The arena could hold 9,000 to 12,000 people for different events. The Amphitheatre was torn down in 1999.

"I went to a ton of Stock Shows at the Amphitheater. As a kid we always got jobs there."

"They use to have great HAUNTED houses at the Amp for Halloween."

"There was always a Rodeo. I remember the Budweiser Horse and Wagon Races. About six wagons would race around the rodeo area. The people loved them!"

Amphitheatre Music Scene

Elvis Presley appeared in 1957 before 12,000 screaming fans. He made his first appearance in his famous $2500 gold jacket.

The Beatles appeared not once, but twice at the Amphitheater. They held concerts in 1964 and 1966. In the '64 concert, the Beatles, while playing before 13,000 fans, were showered with jelly beans after George Harrison mentioned that the 'jelly bean' was one of his favorite foods. Of course, several girls passed out at the concert.

Many other groups appeared at the Amphitheatre such as:
Earth Wind and Fire, Tom Jones, Jackson Five, Rolling Stones,
Liberace, Rush, The Who, KISS and countless more.

*"I loved going to the Amphitheatre to see auto shows, drag racing,
wrestling and rock groups like Mick Jaggar, Pink Floyd and
Stevie Wonder."*

Amphitheatre Barnum and Bailey Circus

The circus was a major event for several decades. Many
remember the circus entourage of performers and animals making
their way through the Bridgeport streets from the train to the
Amphitheatre.

*"My favorite memory was when the Circus would come to town.
They would get off of the trains at Cermak and Archer and all the
animals would make their way down Canal to
26th, to Emerald, to 43rd."*

*"The animals for the circus would pass by my house. I would sit on
my porch thinking, 'how great is this?' as I'd watch them go by."*

"You could pet the animals at the circus. They would have these giant elephants just on a string and would let you pet them."

"I remember one year an elephant turned on the crown and hurt a lot of people."

Amphitheatre Chicago Auto Show

The Chicago Auto show was held annually from 1936 until 1961 at the Amphitheatre. It then switched to the McCormick Place and returned for only a few more years in the late 1960's, when fire had damaged the McCormick Place. The Auto Show continues to be a huge event in Chicago.

Courtesy of the Chicago Auto Show

Amphitheatre Politics

Did you know that the Amphitheater hosted FIVE national conventions? The Republicans held theirs in 1952 when Dwight Eisenhower was nominated the presidential candidate and in 1960 when Richard Nixon was nominated. The Democrats held their conventions in 1952, 1956 and 1968.

1960

Chicago History Museum

Amphitheatre Sports Events

Growing up in Bridgeport, one was lucky to be able to see several pro sports teams play. Some fondly remember the Chicago Cougars hockey team who were a part of the World Hockey League that later merged with the National Hockey League.

Others are shocked to find out that the Chicago Bulls played their first season at the International Amphitheatre. In addition, very few would remember that the first NBA team in Chicago was

NOT the Bulls, but the Chicago Packers who played their first season (1961-62) games at the Amphitheatre.

However, there were many other events held at the Amphitheatre such as the roller derby, and boxing matches including Joe Frazier's last bout in 1981. For many years the Chicago Public League held their basketball championship games there before thousands of fans. Even Evil Knievel performed at the Amphitheatre. Finally, let's not forget pro wrestling or as some would say, "pro wrasslin," which drew big crowds.

"I saw Hulk Hogan verse the Ultimate Warrior at the Amp."

Chicago Cougars

In 1972, a new pro hockey league started called the World Hockey Association (WHA). The league lasted for several seasons before merging with the National Hockey League (NHL). The Chicago Cougars played three seasons at the Amphitheatre from 1972 to 1975. Over 6,000 fans attended the opening home game in 1972. In their second season, the Cougars made it to the WHA championship finals but were swept by the great Gordie Howe and the Houston Aeros.

"We used to go to the Amphitheater to see the Cougars games. Once leaving the Amphitheater we walked down the ramps talking to 'Reggie Fleming' who played for the Cougars and Blackhawks. He recently passed away."

The Chicago Packers

The Chicago Packers were actually Chicago's FIRST NBA team. They played in the NBA for two seasons before moving to Baltimore to become the Baltimore Bullets (now the Washington Wizards).

The Packers played their first season, 1961-62, at the Amphitheatre. The Packers were last in attendance in the league with a little over 2,000 fans per game. Of course, only winning 18 games while losing 62 didn't help!

The team had a monster year by rookie Walt Bellamy who averaged 31 points and 19 rebounds a game! He was voted NBA rookie of the year and went on to a hall of fame career. The next year the team changed their name to the Chicago Zephyrs and moved to the Chicago Coliseum for one season.

Chicago Bulls

The Bulls played their first and only season at the Chicago Amphitheatre during the 1966-67 season. They were an expansion franchise and they went 33-48 and made the NBA playoffs where they lost to the St. Louis Hawks in the first round.

The Bulls averaged a little over 4,000 fans per game. The team was coached by legendary Chicago native, Johnny "Red" Kerr. He was named coach of the year that season. The opening night lineup was: Guy Rodgers, Len Chappell, Bob Boozer, Don Kojis and Jerry Sloan. The Bulls would leave the Amphitheatre the next season to start their long run at the Chicago Stadium.

Comiskey Park

Chicago History Museum **By:Chicago Daily News, 1913**

Comiskey Park was built on a former city dump in 1910 by Charles Comiskey. It held 29,000 which was later expanded and was for several years considered the best ballpark in the American League. The park was torn down in 1991.

Comiskey Park has been associated with Major League Baseball and the NFL with the White Sox and Cardinals. However, Comiskey Park has also hosted a variety of other events. Joe Louis won a heavyweight boxing match at Comiskey in 1937. Pro wrestling also made several ventures. The Beatles performed two concerts there in 1965. Finally, who will ever forget the ***Disco Demolition Night*** at Comiskey Park in 1978?

Comiskey and Pro Sports

Chicago Cardinals

The Chicago Cardinals played NFL football at Comiskey Park for 37 years from 1922-1959. Many old time Bridgeport folks can remember watching the Cards play at Comiskey on a warm fall afternoon or a cold snowy day. The Cardinals were bought by the Bidwell family in 1932 and today the Bidwell family still owns the Cardinals, the Arizona Cardinals.

The Chicago Cardinals struggled for wins and fans for much of their existence. However, the Cards enjoyed two great years in 1947 and 1948. The Cards won the NFL title in 1947 over the Philadelphia Eagles, 28-21. The next year the team went 11-1 but lost the championship to the same Eagle team 7-0 in the famous 'Snow Game' in Philadelphia.

In the 1950's the Cards fell on hard times and only had one winning season the entire decade. One highlight though was in 1953 when the Cardinals, 0-10-1, were playing their arch rivals the *Chicago Bears* at Wrigley Field in the final game of the season. The Cards upset the Bears that day 24-17 to win their only game that year.

Speaking of the Bears, the Cardinals-Bears game was one of the biggest rivalry games in the NFL for three decades. George Halas, owner and coach of the Bears, greatly disliked the Cardinals. As you can imagine, when these two teams met you could forget the records. The game would receive top coverage by the cities newspapers and both Wrigley and Comiskey Park would usually enjoy their biggest crowds of the season. It's sad that such a rivalry does not exist today.

87

After the 1959 season, the Bidwell family moved the Cardinals to St. Louis where they became the St. Louis Cardinals. Later on, the family moved the team to Phoenix where they are currently the Arizona Cardinals. It is interesting to note that that the Cardinals have experienced little success on the field no matter what town they have been in!

The Chicago Cardinals Football team playing in 1959 at Comiskey Park

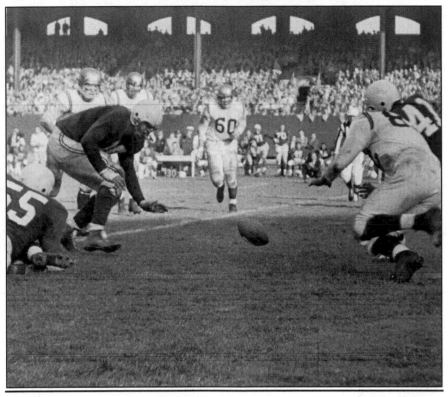

Chicago History Museum, 1959

"I use to sell papers during the White Sox and Chicago Cardinals football games. When it would rain we would yell, "Hey Mister, don't let the lady sit on a wet seat, buy a paper!"

"Growing up in the shadows of Comiskey Park, I was a White Sox and Cardinal Fan. I went to many games. I am still a Cardinal fan even though they moved to St. Louis."

Chicago *Cardinals*

1947 WORLD CHAMPIONS
WESTERN CHAMPIONS 1948

1951 PRESS, RADIO AND TELEVISION GUIDE

Chicago White Sox

No one will ever forget the excitement of 2005 when the Sox won their first World Series championship since 1917. But, growing up in Bridgeport back in the day, the team that many old timers remember is the White Sox World Series team of 1959.

The Go-Go Sox of the Nellie Fox & Louis Aparicio era is still alive in the memories of many. What about such players as Billy Pierce and Minnie Minoso (Sox fan favorites of the 1950's)? Others remember the Sox teams of the 1960's with such players as: Pete Ward, Tommie Agee, Ken Berry, Gary Peters, Hoyt Wilhelm and Walt "no neck" Williams. In the 70's no one can forget the MVP year of Dick Allen, and the play at third base of Bill Melton and manager Chuck Tanner.

Many also have memories of listening on the radio to long time announcer Bob Elson. Elson did exclusive White Sox broadcasts from 1946 to 1970. Also, who can forget the arrival of Harry Carey along with Jimmy Piersall in the 70's? In addition, we cannot forget such fixtures as Andy the Clown and Nancy Faust on the organ who helped usher in the famous Sox song, "Na Na, Hey Hey, Goodbye."

"In 1947, at Comiskey Park, I had my Picture taken with Babe Ruth in a group shot. I was the first kid picked. Babe died a year later."

"No year was more exciting than the 1959 pennant win. The Cleveland Indians were our rivals and every game was so exciting! I remember them carrying in a coffin to one of the games to signify burying the Indians!"

"I remember the sirens going off in 1959 when the Sox won the American league. Some people thought the Russians were attacking!"

"When the Sox won in 1959, People were driving around the neighborhood beeping their horns and yelling."

"My Dad woke us up to tell us the Sox won the pennant in '59 and he hung a flag with all the players names on it over our bed."

White Sox World Series 1959

Chicago History Museum, By: A.A. Novick, 1959 World Series

"My first memory of the White Sox was in 1959 with Jim Landis. I've been a fan ever since. The 1977 " Hit Men" were probably the most exciting. They were amazing hitters but the best team, bar none, was the 2005 team."

Chicago History Museum, Minnie Minoso and Jimmy Adair coach, 1959

Chicago History Museum , 1959, Nellie Fox

93

Comiskey Park 35th and Shields, 1989

Chicago History Museum, By: Tome Harney

"I remember going to Sox Park for just $2.00."

"I was thrilled when Bill Veck asked me to sing the national anthem. (I was dating his son at the time, but it was a thrill none the less.)"

"We use to wait in the parking lot for the Sox players to come out. Once, Early Wynn gave us a lift home to 28th and Shields."

"My brother and I would wait outside the ball park until someone would leave and then ask for their tickets and go back in for the remainder of the game."

"I stabbed my cousin with a pencil once because I was so mad that Mickey Mantle hit a home run in the ninth to beat the Sox. My cousin was a Yankee fan. My mom said, "You could have given him LEAD POISONING!""

"We grew up going to Sox games, sitting in the bleachers, and playing in the shower!"

"All the kids played in the shower!"

"We used to sneak into Comiskey Park when the sox were away and run up and down the ramps until the workers would chase us out."

"I remember sneaking into to Sox Park and roller skating."

"We use to park cars for the baseball games in front of our house for 25 cents a car and then we'd sit on top of the cars and watch the Friday night fireworks."

"How about the "DISCO SUCKS" demolition at Comiskey Park. I was there for the historic blowing up of disco records and I am embarrassed to say that I was one of those rowdy kids scaling the walls and running around the field. I can't believe we cost them to forfeit the game! What were we thinking? [Maybe that we'd go down in HISTORY!]"

"I once saw Paul Newman at Comiskey Park during one of the games. I told my friend, 'Doesn't that look like Paul Newman?' We got a little closer and it was him!"

Music Scene at Comiskey Park

Many concerts had been held at Comiskey Park over the years. In 1978 and 1979 'Summer Jam Concerts' included such bands as Aerosmith and AC/DC. However, perhaps the most famous were the two concerts the Beatles put on in one day in 1965. Between both shows there were 80,000 in attendance!

"When the BEATLES came to Comiskey Park somehow my little brother got me a ticket. I will never forget the girls screaming, crying and fainting!"

The Beatles Performing at Comiskey Park in 1965

Chicago History Museum, Photographer: Chicago Daily News 1965 (Cropped)

Comiskey Park Factoids

The first ever Major League Baseball All-Star game was played at Comiskey in 1933. The park also hosted an All-Star game in 1950 and MLB held the 50th All-Star game anniversary at Comiskey.

The Negro League held many of their All-Star games at Comiskey Park in the 30's, 40's, and 50's.

The largest baseball crowd at Comiskey Park was for a " bat day" game against the Minnesota Twins in 1973 with 55,000 in attendance.

First baseball game played at Comiskey was July 1, 1910 in which they lost to the St. Louis Browns. The last game was September 30, 1990 when the Sox won over the Seattle Mariners.

"Comiskey Park was an icon. It was so original.
I wish they would have left it up."

"Comiskey Park was legend and will never be forgotten!"

"Don't cry because it's over.
Smile because it happened!"
Dr. Seuss

End Notes

Bridgeport facts were gathered from the following sources:

Chapter Two - Theatres
    Cinematreasures.org/theatres
Chapter Three – Parks and Recreation
    Chicago Park District website – www.chicagoparkdistrict
Chapter Four – Schools and Churches
    Wikipedia en.wikipedia.org/wiki/Bridgeport,_Chicago
    Encyclopedia of Chicago - www.encyclopedia.Chicago
    University of Illinois-Chicago Historical Preservation Project
    http://www.uic/edu/orgs/lockzero
Chapter Five – Businesses
    www.schulzeburch.com/about/history
Chapter Seven – Iconic Places
    en.wikipedia.org/wiki/union_stock_yards
    en.wikipedia.org/wiki/International_Amphitheatre
    en.wikipedia.org/wiki/Chicago_Cougars
    www.Chicagocougars.net
    www.absoluteastronomy.com/topics/comiskey
    www.basketball-reference.com/teams
    www.sportsencyclopedia
    www.sportsencyclopeda

Thank You

I would like to thank all of those who have helped make this book possible. Many of you are from our church, while many others took time to fill out survey forms and to share memories that we can all relate to.

I would also like to thank those who donated photos, as well as the Chicago History Museum for their help with pictures. All of your input has helped to make this book complete and full of lasting ***"Bridgeport Memories!"***

****

Books available through
Central Assembly of God
816 W. 31st
Chicago, Il 60608
312-326-1818
centralassembly@rocketmail.com
Website: ccaog.com

****

An added thank you to the following for their help in gathering memories:

Rose and Bob Allen, Debbie and Vince Vanaria, Donna and Joe Battaglia, Judy and Don Weingatner, Mary Caponigro, Lisa, Montesano, Pam Mangan, Norma Marcotte, Peter Gains, Joseph and Eileen Kraslen, Jim Loughney, Florence Tucker, Lyndie, March, Charles Pizzurro, Jose Ramos, Blanca Orsorio, Jean Vicaria, Elena Reed, Barbara Alberts, Josie Nations, Joann Kratina Racevice, Diana Campbell, Nadine Pajauskas Downs and Fran Sabia

A special thank you to Ginny Caponigro for sorting through all that was submitted, and making a book out of it.